by
Jon
Allison

Parachute Press, Inc.
156 Fifth Avenue
New York, New York 10010

ISBN: 0-938753-70-3

First Printing: September 1992
Printed in the USA

Design by Elizabeth Sheehan Graphic Design

COVER PHOTO CREDITS

David Robinson
© David L. Johnson/Sports Chrome

Magic Johnson
© Jeff Carlick/Sports Chrome East/West

Patrick Ewing
© Scott Cunningham/Focus on Sports

Michael Jordan
© Focus on Sports

Larry Bird
© Jerry Wachter/Focus on Sports

Charles Barkley
© Jerry Wachter/Focus on Sports

Table of CONTENTS

Chapter One:
The American Game........................5

Chapter Two:
The Pros for Barcelona....................10

Chapter Three:
Patrick Ewing 14

Chapter Four:
Michael "Air" Jordan 20

Chapter Five:
Magic!—Magic Johnson 25

Chapter Six:
Karl "The Mailman" Malone 30

Chapter Seven:
The Round Mound—Charles Barkley 34

Chapter Eight:
The Hired Gun—Chris Mullin 49

Chapter Nine:
Slick from French Lick—Larry Bird 54

Chapter Ten:
The Admiral—David Robinson 58

Chapter Eleven:
Out of the Shadows—Scottie Pippen 64

Chapter Twelve:
Mr. Point Guard—John Stockton........... 69

Chapter Thirteen:
**In the Pressure Cooker—
Coach Chuck Daly 74**

Chapter Fourteen:
**The Bonus Picks — Clyde Drexler and
Christian Laettner......................... 77**

Chapter Fifteen:
Staying Home 81

Chapter Sixteen:
What Next?................................ 84

Chapter Seventeen:
Player Stats 90

The American Game

As the newscasters might say, December 21, 1891, was just another day. Except that in Springfield, Massachusetts, a physical-education professor named James Naismith happened to be very busy that day. Dr. Naismith's boss had asked him to come up with a new indoor activity to keep his students busy during the long, cold New England winter. Naismith had already tried a number of things, including indoor soccer, indoor lacrosse, and indoor rugby. But none of those sports had drummed up much enthusiasm.

The good doctor was fast running out of ideas when he nailed a peach basket to each of two balconies at opposite ends of the YMCA gym and told his students to toss a ball into the baskets. That day, a great new American game was born. Naismith's students wanted to call it Naismithball, but on second thought, basketball was deemed a better name.

Naismith's game quickly became popular throughout the United States as college teams started competing against each other. Within a couple of years, someone had substituted an iron rim and a net for the peach basket, and in 1896 the first Championship of America took place—the winners outscoring the losers, 4-0.

Word of the great new game began to spread around the world, but for the most part it remained the American game. The U.S. team played Olympic exhibitions (games where no medals were awarded) in 1904, and again in 1924, 1928, and 1932. Finally, in 1936, there was enough international interest in the sport to make it an official Olympic event. Not surprisingly, the United States won.

Starting with that 19-8 gold-medal victory over Canada on a muddy outdoor court in Berlin, American teams tore through eight Olympics from 1936 to 1972. Until the 1972 Games, the United States not only won every gold medal—it won every one of its games. And only a few of the games were even close. In the 1948 Finals, the U.S.A. celebrated a 65-21 victory over France, and in the 1956 Finals, an 89-55 victory over the U.S.S.R.

During World War II, American soldiers stationed abroad played basketball all over the world, and that's when the sport really caught on internationally. The U.S.S.R. entered the Olympics in 1952 and within a few years became the United States' chief rival. But even then America continued to dominate the game. In 1956, at Melbourne, the great Bill Russell led the United States to victory in the final game. And in 1960, Oscar Robertson and Jerry West were just two players on what may have been the greatest Olympic team ever.

Then, in 1972, things began to change. Some controversial calls in one game gave the Soviets three chances at the gold medal, and they finally won it on the third try with a score of 51-50. The U.S. streak—63 straight wins in eight Olympics—was broken, as the gold departed for Moscow.

The United States regained the first place medal in 1976 by routing Yugoslavia in the final game, 95-74, after almost losing to Puerto Rico in an early round. And in 1980, the American team didn't play after President Jimmy Carter called for a boycott of the Olympics to protest the Soviet invasion of Afghanistan. Four years later in 1984 the United States, led by college stars Michael Jordan, Chris Mullin, and Patrick Ewing, won easily—but this time the Soviets weren't there. Neither were Bulgaria and Cuba, both major rivals. The Communist countries boycotted the Games. By 1988, all the big basketball powers were back on the court and the U.S. had to settle for the third-place bronze medal, behind the U.S.S.R. and Yugoslavia.

American basketball fans thought their team should have finished first. "These other countries," they complained, "are using all of their best players, calling them amateurs, while we admit that our best players are pros. If we could use our real pros against their so-called amateurs, you'd see the difference."

Leaders of USA Basketball, the official governing body of amateur basketball in the United States, knew the fans had a point. For the first 56 years of Olympic basketball, the Americans had been very successful with non-professionals, who were still far ahead of anyone else's pros. The Americans were so good that it didn't even seem to matter that the U.S. Olympic team was never assembled until the final weeks before the Games—unlike the Europeans who played together year-round.

Sometimes, American coaches took whole college teams as units to the Olympics. The University of Kentucky furnished much of the roster in the 1948 Games. Even when the American team was made up of various college all-stars who were little more than strangers to each other, they still managed to win the gold.

But as the 20th century was racing to an end, the old system of amateurs versus pros wasn't working. The rest of the world had finally caught up to, and was even surpassing, America's amateurs. There was only one solution. On April 7, 1989, FIBA, the international governing body of basketball, announced that any player—amateur or pro—could now compete in the Olympic Games.

How would America's best do against the world's best? Just imagine the likes of Magic Johnson and Michael Jordan and Larry Bird on the same team, not just for one all-star game, but for an entire Olympics match. If players such as Patrick Ewing and David Robinson and Karl Malone were hitting the boards for the U.S., would any rebound escape their clutches? And what if you needed a three-point shot? Could you miss if you had Michael or Larry or Chris Mullin to call on?

The 1992 U.S. Olympic basketball team was really going to be a Dream Team, with the greatest American talent all working together at the same time. For basketball fans, it just couldn't get any better than this.

The Pros for Barcelona

Having America's best at the 1992 Olympics drove basketball experts and fans wild. But there were questions. Lots of questions.

The United States has so many great basketball players, how do you pick just 12? Choosing 24 players for the NBA All-Stars every February is tough enough. There always were fans who were enraged when their favorite player wasn't selected. And sometimes players weren't too happy either!

But the Olympic roster needed only 12 players. Oh, sure, Michael Jordan was a must. So was Magic Johnson. But who would play the point guard—Isiah Thomas or John Stockton? Isiah was a better shooter while Stockton was the premier passer. And when the "pro" Olympics were announced, Scottie Pippen was just coming into his own with the Chicago Bulls. By selection time, he was becoming a superstar. The job of picking America's Dream Team wasn't going to be easy.

In the meantime, the rest of the world couldn't wait for the Games. In hoop-crazy countries like Spain and Italy, the Commonwealth of Independent States (formerly the U.S.S.R.) and Yugoslavia, and Brazil and Argentina, fans waited anxiously. The chance to see their local heroes matched up against their long-distance heroes, the American pros, was the greatest thing to happen to basketball fans anywhere. But to the people who had to choose the American "twelve," the Dream Team might start to look more like a nightmare.

In previous years, the U.S. Olympic Team was selected after a series of practices and games known as the Olympic Trials. But this year, USA Basketball created a special committee to choose its Olympians. That way, the try-outs wouldn't have to be held in the less-than-two-week period between June 14, the end of the 1992 NBA Finals, and June 27, the start of the Olympic qualifying tournament.

Officially known as the Men's Olympic Team Subset, the committee was chaired by the University of Kentucky's athletic director, C. M. Newton. On February 15, 1991, the Subset appointed the coach for the U.S. team, Chuck Daly of the Detroit Pistons. Chuck, who had already coached winners at the high school, college, and pro levels, was a perfect choice. Two months later, the assistant coaches were named: Duke's Mike Krzyewski, Seton Hall's P. J. Carlesimo, and the Cleveland Cavaliers' Len Wilkens.

Basketball fans then turned their attention to the athletes. Who would get the call? The Subset announced that it would name ten players, holding spots 11 and 12 until just a few months before the Games. At least one, perhaps two, of those spots would go to collegians.

Who were the best players for the job? Opinions naturally varied, but almost everybody agreed that Michael Jordan should be on the team. Everybody, that is, but Michael. "I play hard for nine months for the Bulls," he told the press. "During the summer, I want to forget basketball and concentrate on golf. Besides, I already have an Olympic gold medal."

Basketball fans and experts knew that a team without "Air" Jordan wouldn't be America's best. A great deal of pressure, much of it from Magic Johnson, was applied to the Chicago superstar. Finally, he changed his mind.

On September 21, 1991, the official 1992 U.S. team was announced:

- Patrick Ewing, New York Knicks
- Michael Jordan, Chicago Bulls
- Earvin "Magic" Johnson,
  Los Angeles Lakers
- Karl Malone, Utah Jazz

- Charles Barkley, Philadelphia 76ers
- Chris Mullin, Golden State Warriors
- Larry Bird, Boston Celtics
- David Robinson, San Antonio Spurs
- Scottie Pippen, Chicago Bulls
- John Stockton, Utah Jazz

Then on May 11, 1992, Clyde Drexler of the Portland Trail Blazers and Christian Laettner of Duke University were added to the team. With the exception of Laettner, the roster was a veritable Who's Who of the NBA, but not everyone was satisfied with every choice. Where was Isiah Thomas? some fans wanted to know. And what about Detroit's Dennis Rodman, the premier defensive star and rebounder? Still others complained that some college stars would miss out on a once-in-a-lifetime chance to play in the Olympics because of the new no-Trials, all-pro arrangement.

The process, however, was now complete. Few folks who've ever seen a basketball game could argue that the 1992 Olympic Team was comprised of the greatest collection of talent ever to play together. As the rest of the world got ready for the U.S. invasion of Barcelona, the rim-rocking, play-above-the-hoop, in-your-face Americans prepared to show everyone how far Dr. Naismith's peach-basket game had come in its first 100 years.

PATRICK EWING

The New York Knicks' monster center was born in Jamaica, where he spent much of his childhood playing soccer. If the late Dorothy Ewing hadn't had a dream, her son Patrick might have come to the Olympics as a member of that Caribbean island's soccer team instead of the U.S. basketball team.

But Patrick's mom dreamed of a better life for her family, and moved to the United States, later sending for her husband and children with the money she earned working in the kitchen of a Boston hospital. That's how a 12-year-old Patrick Ewing, who'd never seen a basketball before, came to Cambridge, Massachusetts.

Even then, Patrick was tall for his age, and once he started playing this new game, it didn't take him long to get going. By the time he arrived at Rindge & Latin High School in Cambridge two years later in 1977, he was already 6 feet 6 inches tall. Patrick moved right in as the starting center, but in his first game he was held to a grand total of one point! Over the next four years, however, he added 1,762 points to that total—including 41 in his last outing—as he led his school to three straight Massachusetts state championships. In fact, after his junior year, Ewing became the first high-school hoopster ever invited to the U.S. Olympic Trials.

From there it was on to college, after a very careful recruiting process. Sixteen schools had been invited to make presentations to the Ewing family and advisors in Cambridge. The Ewings were most impressed with Georgetown's coach, John Thompson, a 6-foot 11-inch tower of a man who had once played for the Boston Celtics.

Everyone knew Patrick could score, but at Georgetown he also became a tiger on defense. Opponents knew that when they flashed into the paint, Ewing would be there to stop them. At 7 feet tall, Patrick was an undeniably imposing presence. Three times he led the Hoyas to the NCAA championship finals and, in 1984, to the championship itself. Playing at the top of his game, Patrick was the tournament MVP.

That summer, coach Bobby Knight picked Ewing for the 1984 U.S. Olympic Team. It was an all-star group that included Michael Jordan, Chris Mullin, and Sam Perkins. With the Soviet team at home in its Olympic boycott, the U.S. squad easily won the gold, topping Spain, 96-65, in the final. Patrick led the tournament with 18 blocked shots, averaging 11 points and 5.6 rebounds per game.

Ewing wound up his Hoya career at the end of the 1985 season as the most sought-after college athlete in the nation. He was what the pros call a franchise player, the kind who can turn a team around all by himself.

The NBA chose 1985 to introduce its new draft lottery system. Previously, only the two teams with the league's worst records had a chance to compete (it was a coin toss) for the rights to the top college pick. But now all of the league's seven non-playoff teams would have a shot as the NBA commissioner picked cards "out of the hat" on national TV.

The Knicks were the lucky team. Ewing would play in New York—where he was badly needed. The home team had been losing big and the fans had been staying away in droves. With the prospect of Ewing suddenly a reality, by the following morning Knicks backers were lining up at the box office for season tickets.

Though Ewing didn't bring any titles to Madison Square Garden, he didn't let anyone down either, in spite of personal challenges. The first couple of years, he suffered with injuries that cost him a lot of playing time. In his rookie season alone, an elbow injury, a twisted ankle, and a sprained knee sidelined him for 32 games.

Still he was named the NBA's Rookie of the Year, with an average of 20 points and 9 rebounds per game. Included in those credentials was an incredible Christmas Day performance televised nationally. Thanks to Patrick, the Knicks upset the eventual champion Boston Celtics in two overtimes. But even Ewing couldn't help the Knicks finish better than a dismal 23-59 for the season.

The following year a new experiment began. Bill Cartwright, the Knicks' center before Ewing arrived, returned to the line-up after missing two full seasons. Cartwright could only play center, so Patrick was forced to move to power forward, not the greatest of moves. Ewing had never played facing the basket. The Knicks continued to lose. Then New York started playing "musical coaches," sacking both Hubie Brown and Bob Hill. Still, Patrick kept scoring, averaging 21.5 points per game with 8.7 rebounds.

That's when Rick Pitino took over as coach —great news for Ewing. As a kid in Cambridge, Patrick had often dropped in to watch the Boston University Terriers practice. Pitino was then the Terriers' coach.

Now, ten years later, Pitino brought his wide-open style featuring a pressing defense to New York. With Patrick leading the club, the new approach turned things around. The Knicks improved to 38-44, tying with the Washington Bullets for second best in the Atlantic Division.

Injury-free at last, Patrick finally got to play in every game and averaged 20.2 points per game—not as high as his pre-injury average—but only because his teammates had improved their game and were scoring more.

The 1988-89 Knicks won the Atlantic Division, racking up an impressive 52-30 record. With Cartwright gone to Chicago (Charles Oakley came in return), Patrick returned to his favorite spot, down low and with his back to the basket. That season he ranked among the NBA's top 20 in scoring (22.7), rebounding (9.2), and shooting (74.6%). If anyone ever had any doubts about Patrick Ewing as a franchise player, those doubts were gone forever. Whenever a team played against the Knicks, the first thing it had to do was figure out how to stop Ewing.

The Knicks struggled after Pitino decided to leave New York for the University of Kentucky. Even Patrick couldn't save the team as it started going through coaches again, quickly dispatching Stu Jackson and John McLeod, who actually left before the Knicks had a chance to fire him. But Patrick kept right on going. In 1989-90, he finished third in scoring (28.6) and fifth in rebounding (10.9) in the NBA. Along the way, he turned in one spectactular 44-point, 24-rebound performance against Golden State. Then, in the first round of the NBA playoffs, after the Knicks had lost the first two games of a best-of-five series against their arch rivals, the Boston Celtics, Patrick brought them back from the dead with another 44 points in a Game 4 victory, and 31 more in the final game at the Boston Garden. Unfortunately, the highlights were too few and far between. The Knicks were blown out by Detroit in the next round.

The 1990-91 season was even worse. The Knicks dipped back to 39-43 and made a quick playoff exit, losing three straight to the eventual champion Chicago Bulls. But Patrick tried to stay at the top of his form, placing fifth in the league both in scoring (26.6) and rebounding (11.2).

In 1991-92, the Knicks talked about trading their superstar, but lucky for them, they were unable to complete a deal. Ewing proved to be priceless. Surrounded by a new cast of players and a new coach—former Laker boss Pat Riley—Patrick was better than ever, and the Knicks zoomed right back to the top of the Atlantic Division.

What makes Patrick Ewing so great? His size, of course, and his incredible ability to run the floor. His shooting range has expanded out beyond the 15-foot range and his shot-blocking skills continue to improve. But most important is Patrick's great intensity. No one, it seems, wants to win more than he does, and no one is more willing to work toward that goal.

MICHAEL "Air" JORDAN

To basketball fans from Chicago to Chattanooga to Katmandu, Michael means one thing: Michael Jordan. Some people think that Jordan may well be bigger than the game itself. His every move, his every word draw attention everywhere. When Michael uses Nike shoes, millions of fans rush out and buy them. When Michael drinks Gatorade, people all around the world start gulping down the stuff. As one of the commercials says, lots of folks "want to be like Mike." He's probably the planet's most famous athlete.

Although the 1992 U.S. Olympic hoop roster was loaded with stars, there's no doubt that Michael shone the brightest. But months before the U.S. team was announced, it was reported that Jordan didn't want to take part.

"That simply wasn't true," answers Michael. "I had already made my decision, but I wanted to keep it low key. I knew all along I wanted to play."

Though Michael didn't make his high school team at Laney High in Wilmington, North Carolina, until his junior year, he always wanted to play. And he played well enough to earn a scholarship offer from the University of North Carolina's Dean Smith—among many others.

At UNC, where the school song might as well be "Team! Team! Team!," Jordan fit right in. Although he averaged only 13.5 points per game in his 1981 freshman year, the last two of his 460 points that season were the biggest. North Carolina was trailing Georgetown, 62-61, with only 16 seconds left in the NCAA final, when Michael shot a tough 17-footer from the left side (yes, his tongue was sticking out even then), to give the Tarheels a one point victory over Georgetown—and Patrick Ewing. To this day it remains the team's only national title.

After three seasons at North Carolina, Michael had earned a 17.7 points per game average, two college Player of the Year titles, and a berth on the gold-medal 1984 U.S. Olympic team. Still, the 1984 season produced his biggest disappointment, a loss to Indiana in the Eastern Regionals, which cost UNC another national title.

That's when Jordan decided he'd had enough of college basketball. The Bulls leaped at the chance to let him lead them. Instead of playing his senior year at North Carolina, Michael went to Chicago on the third pick of the NBA draft, and he's never looked back.

Freed from the limitations of Coach Smith's offensive plan, Michael bloomed overnight. It quickly became apparent that there wasn't another player in the game who could keep him from scoring. Whether he was popping them in from the outside or twisting, floating, hanging in the air before a mind-bending layup or slam dunk, Jordan defied every law—including gravity. The basketball phrase "go-to guy" could have been invented to describe Michael Jordan. When the going got tough, he was always the one they'd go to.

Michael was a shoo-in as the NBA's Rookie of the Year, and his fame soon spread far beyond the basketball court. Nike signed Michael and agreed to manufacture a special line of Air Jordan shoes. Though the NBA tried to ban the unique-looking sneakers from their courts, they still sold like hotcakes. It helped make Michael the world's richest athlete.

Meanwhile, back on the courts, if it's Michael's offense that sells tickets and thrills fans, it's his defense that makes him the premier star that he is. No one works harder on the defensive end than Jordan. He was voted the NBA's Defensive Player of the Year in 1988 and he made the All-Defense team five times in a row. You simply don't get a freebie against Michael. With his super quickness, unrelenting pressure, and great hands, opponents really have to work hard to get an open shot.

Everyone in the game raves about Jordan. Listen to what L.A. Clippers coach Larry Brown, an old Tarheel himself, has to say: "There's no question. Michael is the best. I grew up with some great players. I saw Julius Erving at his peak. I love Magic and Larry. But I'd pay serious money to watch Michael play... and I don't make that statement often."

Still, for all his greatness, Michael missed out on the biggest prize—an NBA title—until 1991. Then, after watching the Detroit Pistons take two straight championships, Jordan, Scottie Pippin, and the rest of the Bulls finally put it together. Michael averaged more than 31 points, 7 rebounds, 11 assists, and 2 steals in leading Chicago to an almost painless victory over the western champion L.A. Lakers. "I've gotta tip my hat to Michael," raved Magic Johnson, leader of the loyal opposition. "He did a great job."

The big question in '92 was just how long Jordan would keep doing that job. Michael's current contract expires after the 1995 season. "I'm thinking about retiring at that time," Michael recently said, but many fans and experts doubt he'll be ready to pack it in at the age of 32. True, he doesn't exactly need the money. These days, Michael earns about $25 million a year, most of it from non-basketball activities. But what about the priceless pleasures of dominating the sport he so clearly loves? Will he be ready to give that up?

If Jordan runs true to form, chances are he'll keep his decision private until the opening tip in November 1995.

MAGIC!—MAGIC JOHNSON

Earvin Johnson, Jr., is what it says on his birth certificate. But to anyone who hasn't spent the last 13 years on a far-off desert island or in a remote cave, he's just plain Magic. The mile-wide smile. The winning personality. The smooth-as-silk performance on the court. That's what makes Johnson so magical.

While he was in high school (Everett High in Lansing, Michigan), Johnson improved his basketball skills by hanging around the playgrounds with older players. Soon he was outplaying them. Would-be stars from all over the state heard about Earvin, and some would drive for hours for a chance to take on Johnson and his crew at Lansing's basketball haven, Main Street Park. "They wanted to beat us—and steal our girlfriends," Magic recalls. "We couldn't let that happen."

By Magic's senior year (1976-77), Everett

High had one of the best teams in the state. With Earvin in the lead, Everett captured the Michigan state title right across town at the University of Michigan's arena.

Johnson's college choice was easy. He wanted to play for Michigan State, in East Lansing, so that his family could watch him in action every time he played. And just as important, the Spartans were building a major program under veteran coach Jud Heathcote. Magic Johnson was all it needed to go all the way.

The 1979 NCAA championship game was one of the most eagerly anticipated ever. The power of the Big Ten would be matched against unbeaten but unknown Indiana State, a test that would pit Magic Johnson against Larry Bird. Bird came up big, but Magic's more talented team came up even bigger. Round one of the long series of head-to-head matchups went to Magic.

When the season ended, Johnson announced that he would turn pro after only two years in college. Despite his relative inexperience, the L.A. Lakers used their number-one draft pick to snap him up.

Los Angeles was the perfect spot for the 20-year-old. With Kareem Abdul-Jabbar at center and plenty of other talent all around, Magic fit in immediately. Some people thought that at 6 feet 9 inches he wouldn't be quick enough to play point guard in the pros. They were wrong. Magic led his new team to victory in its opening game and then led an exuberant on-court celebration. "Be cool," Abdul-Jabbar told him. "We still have another 81 games to go." But Magic wasn't cool; he was red-hot.

Somehow Magic managed to get his boundless enthusiasm under control without losing his edge. Every game brought some new move from the youngster who for all time changed the way basketball teams ran their offense. By season's end, the Lakers were on top in the West, with only Philadelphia's superb 76ers standing in the way of an NBA title.

L.A. was up three games to two when center Kareem Abdul-Jabbar was injured and had to be taken out of the lineup. But coach Paul Westhead didn't panic. He simply moved Johnson to center. A point guard playing center? You bet. Even though the Sixers had two of the league's best shot-blockers—Darryl Dawkins and Caldwell Jones—Magic was simply too quick for them. His spinning moves on the inside stunned the Philly defense and his deft passing freed Jamaal Wilkes and Norm Nixon for the long jumpers. Johnson's own 42 points helped salt away the Laker victory and the title. Johnson, who averaged 18.8 points and 10.2 rebounds for the series, was voted the MVP of the playoffs, an unheard-of honor for a rookie.

In a span of only four seasons, Johnson had

won a state high-school championship, an NCAA title, and an NBA crown. No one, before or since, has ever come close.

But it was Magic's attitude, as much as his skill, that made him so beloved by players and fans alike. His super smile was infectious. Magic loved playing the game and everyone knew it. He wrote his name in the record book countless times. He won the league's MVP and playoff MVP awards three times each, he was a first-team All-NBA star eight times. He brought five titles to the Great Western Forum in Los Angeles, and he was a perennial league leader in assists and steals. Those are just some of the reasons the world was devastated when Magic announced in November 1991 that he had contracted the HIV virus that leads to AIDS and would retire. Telecasts were interrupted to feature the tragic story, and newspapers covered the story on their front pages. Even the President of the United States took special notice. But it was Magic himself who made the bad news easier to take. His playing days might soon be over, he said, but he had big plans for his future.

"I am going to be a spokesman for the disease," he told the world. And he has proceeded to be just that. On television and in personal appearances, Magic brought the message about the AIDS virus to young people everywhere. And as an appointee to President Bush's special task force on AIDS, Magic has continued to serve as a spokesman against AIDS.

And there still is some basketball left in the Magic man. Even though he had officially retired, his fans voted him to the starting lineup for the West team in the 1992 NBA All-Star Game. With his doctors' blessing, he brought his act back to the court with all of the gusto that made him Magic. He wound up as the leading scorer and Most Valuable Player. If the Olympics were to be his last hurrah, he would be leaving the game with class and style. And those, after all, were among the many fine qualities he'd entered basketball with.

KARL "The Mailman" MALONE

For years, Utah's Karl Malone was the NBA's best-kept secret. Blame it on geography. With superstars like Magic in Los Angeles, Michael in Chicago, and Patrick in New York—each city a media capital—the Salt Lake City superman was lucky even to be mentioned when hoop fans got together to discuss the game's top pros.

That was nothing new for the muscular Malone, who has always played far from the public eye. Karl grew up in Summerfield, Louisiana, not exactly the crossroads of the high-school basketball world. Few big-time scouts ever passed through, and Malone had to scramble for a scholarship. He wound up at Louisiana Tech, in Ruston, Louisiana, again far off the beaten track. Add to that the fact that the school forced Karl to sit out his freshman year because of low grades (a school requirement), and you might get the idea that it wouldn't be easy for him to make his mark.

And of course, you'd be wrong. When he finally did get to play, Karl was averaging 20.9 points and more than 10 rebounds per game and the word began to go out from Ruston. In fact, Malone spent a month following his sophomore year trying out for the 1984 U.S. Olympic Team. When he didn't make it, he was disappointed—*and* determined. "The Olympic coaches made a mistake," he declared. "And I'm going to prove it!"

The following spring in March 1985, Malone wrapped up his college career with an 18.7 scoring average and a 56.6% shooting mark. His junior year was a high-water mark for his little-known Tech Bulldogs. Thanks largely to Malone, they earned the school's first-ever Top Ten ranking and a berth in the Midwest Regional Finals in Dallas. Pretty heady stuff.

But Karl had had enough. With a year of college eligibility still to go, he decided to make himself eligible for the NBA draft. The Utah Jazz took him on, tapping him as the 13th choice on the first round. They never regretted it.

Even playing in one of the NBA's smaller markets, Malone made an instant impact. Averaging more than 30 minutes per game in 81 contests—a ton of time for a rookie—Karl tossed in 14.9 points per game and grabbed a total of 718 rebounds. If there was a weakness in his arsenal, it was his free throw shooting. Strange as it seems, Malone actually shot better with a man in his face (49.6%) than he did from the foul line (48.1%).

Still, Malone made the NBA All-Rookie team in 1986, and within three seasons he had become an All-Star game regular, an All-NBA defender, and an All-NBA star. And by the 1988-89 season, he had become a solid 76% foul shooter.

If there were any questions about Malone's ability, they were answered at the 1989 All-Star Game. The Jazz star tossed in 28 points and grabbed 13 rebounds. And he picked the perfect time and place to do it—on prime-time TV! Few fans, except those with satellite dishes, ever got to see Karl or the Jazz in action. On All-Star Sunday, however, Karl grabbed the attention of fans across the country.

"Did you see that?" raved the 76ers' outspoken player Charles Barkley. "If you've watched Malone, you've got to know this guy is a monster player." And when the Olympic squad was announced two years later, Malone and Barkley found they'd be playing together.

"It's a real thrill to be representing my country," Malone said when he heard the news. "That's not enough, of course. There's only one reason to go and that's to bring home the gold."

It was no surprise that Malone was tapped for Olympic duty. A career 26-point scorer, Karl parlays tremendous leaping ability with the kind of strength that allows him to keep his opponent off the boards with one hand while grabbing rebounds with the other. "Karl simply never gives up," to quote Olympic coach Chuck Daly.

That's what has made Malone a better player with each passing year. It shows up in virtually every category on the Jazz stat sheet, starting with his incredible climb in free throw shooting. His shooting from field has also improved. Since his sophomore season, he has gone over 50% every year.

Malone's fans are fond of calling him by his boyhood nickname, "The Mailman," earned on the Louisiana schoolyards where he first learned his craft. The name was a tribute to the fact that, like the mailman, Karl Malone always delivers. And as Jazz fans are happy to say, he still does.

The Round Mound— CHARLES BARKLEY

None of the NBA stars chosen for the 1992 U.S. Olympic Team appreciated it more than Charles Barkley. After being snubbed by coach Bob Knight and the Olympic staff in 1984, Barkley had complained that he'd been "robbed." Never dreaming that pros would one day be welcomed into the world competition, he'd held out little hope for another chance. When it came in 1992, he was thrilled. And—true to form—he said so.

Barkley has yet to form an opinion he's afraid to express. Outspoken is a mild word to describe Charles. Almost no one is exempt from his frequent outbursts. As a result, Barkley himself is often a target for verbal abuse from others —especially rival fans. Though it sometimes appears that his mouth runs just a little faster than his brain, the good in Barkley usually outweighs the bad.

"I'm delighted to be going to the Olympics," he said after his selection in September 1991. "I'm going to look at it as just another basketball tournament. But if I have a chance to get some people excited about other issues, like education and drug abuse, I'm certainly going to do it."

Throughout his undergraduate years at Leeds (Alabama) High School and Auburn University, the 290-pound Charles was known as the "Round Mound of Rebound." Though he's down to around 255 pounds these days, at Auburn he outweighed everyone on the Tigers football team. The weight never seemed to bother him, however. He simply occupied more space on the court. Shooting 63.6% throughout his college career, he led the Southeastern Conference in rebounding in each of the three seasons he played. In 1990, he was voted the SEC's Player of the Decade.

The Philadelphia 76ers used their first-round draft pick (the fifth choice overall) on the Round Mound and quickly worked him into the starting lineup.

"What a great way to break in," says Barkley. "Julius Erving was there to do the scoring, and Moses Malone took care of the boards. I had a chance to learn and grow." In fact, it was Malone who became Barkley's role model. "First, Moses taught me how to work hard," says Charles. "Second, he showed me all of the tricks."

Though Barkley never averaged more than 15.1 points per game in college, he quickly became a supershooter in the pros. He may have been listed as 6 feet 6 inches in NBA programs, but insiders knew he was a couple of shades under 6 feet 5 inches. That made his rim-rocking slams even more remarkable—they were shorter and broader than most rim-rockers. After averaging 14 points in his rookie year, he hit the 20 points-per-game mark the next year and hasn't dropped below that since.

"I know everybody looks to me as the leader of the Sixers," says Barkley, "but I never intentionally sought that role. Most of the time, the best player winds up leading his team. I play hard and try to get my teammates to play hard. If people want to call me the leader, I'll accept it. But I truly believe that a leader leads by example—period."

Charles has won virtually every honor the game has to offer. A perennial All-Star, he earned the game's MVP Award in 1991. And he has been an All-NBA first-teamer five times. Still, he would trade all of those individual honors for one NBA championship. The Sixers just missed out during his first season, losing the Eastern title to the Celtics, but they haven't even come close since.

"I can't think of anything more important than winning it all as a team," says Charles. "God gave me a special gift and, for me, unless I get the big prize, I'll always be thinking about what might have been."

When his former coach, Matt Goukas, talks about Charles Barkley, he has only good words to say. "Charles is the kind of player every coach wants," says Goukas, now with the Orlando Magic. "He's certainly one of the four or five best in the league. Sure he'll speak out at a moment's notice, but that's part of what keeps him pumping."

Still, it's difficult to understand some of Barkley's on- and off-court actions. In recent seasons, he has berated Sixers coach Jim Lynam in front of teammates, spat into the crowd at the Nets' Meadowlands Arena, and squared off against Detroit toughguy Bill Laimbeer. "Some of the fans make things very tough," says Barkley. "I don't go to the arena thinking 'What am I going to do to upset someone tonight?' But the fans think they can do or say anything they want to, and that's just wrong. Some guy yells insults and racial slurs at me for four quarters. Then, if I say something back, everyone in his section writes a letter. That isn't the way it should be.

"I may not present a picture of stability to the press and fans, but I am a stable guy. My job is playing basketball and sometimes, in the heat of battle, I get emotional. I do my job well, so I'm not going to apologize for getting hot."

Barkley's performance speaks for itself. A 26 points-per-game scorer, he is always among the league's top ten in rebounding. In fact, in 1987 he won the title with 994 rebounds in only 68 games. And when a guy can do that, it's hard to deny that actions speak louder than words.

On June 17, 1992, the Sixers shipped their outspoken forward to the Phoenix Suns in exchange for three players. It looks like Barkley will have his season in the sun!

© Rob Shanahan/Sports Chrome

No surprise to Barkley fans, Philadelphia 76ers Charles Barkley is a fierce fighter against the Yankee Clippers.

Larry Bird of the Boston Celtics works his way around the Atlanta Hawks on his way to the basket during the 1986 NBA Playoffs.

Chicago Bulls' Michael "Air" Jordan defies gravity to win the 1988 NBA slam-dunk contest.

Scottie Pippen, the "other star" of the Chicago Bulls, sails in for a lay-up over Houston Rockets' Purvis Short in this 1989 game. Pippen's teammate, mega-star Michael Jordan, has his eye on the ball.

Fifty is the number on Dave Robinson's Navy jersey, and the incredible number of points Robinson scored against Michigan in this 1987 college game. Seven-foot one-inch Robinson was the greatest star in Navy history, and consistently burns up the court in the NBA.

© Noren Trotman/Sports Photo Masters

John Stockton of the Utah Jazz declares war on the Golden State Warriors. Once just a skinny little kid, Stockton is now worth his weight in gold to the Jazz.

Karl Malone of the Utah Jazz slam dunks for two of the 28 points he scored in the 1989 All-Star Game, as Charles Barkley of the 76ers watches the action.

Chris Mullin of the Golden State Warriors shows his determination playing against Magic Johnson of the Los Angeles Lakers.

Patrick Ewing of the New York Knicks collides with the Detroit Piston's Bill Laimbeer.

Duke University's Christian Laettner holds off St. John's in the final game of the 1991 ACC Big East Challenge. Duke came out on top with a final score of 91–81.

Everything stops as Clyde Drexler of the Portland Trail-blazers plays 'wait for the drop' against the Bullets.

© Noren Trotman/Sports Photo Masters

1992 U.S. Olympic basketball coach Chuck Daly.

The Hired Gun—CHRIS MULLIN

How do you build a great basketball team? Piece by piece, of course. Every player, even the superstar, is a role player. On any given night, any player may be called upon to step up and take over.

That's what the U.S. Olympic selection committee had in mind when it named Golden State's Chris Mullin to the 1992 squad. The committee realized that sometimes in the course of the tournament the leaders of the inside game—Patrick Ewing, Karl Malone, Charles Barkley—will most likely run into a rival roadblock. And when they do, Mullin will become the key man.

"I wasn't certain that I'd be one of the ten," said Mullin, not long after the announcement was made. "I knew they would look at the top six or seven in each conference before making their picks. And I knew that I'd be one of the top six or seven in the West. But I knew it was a numbers game and I wasn't sure that they'd rank me high enough to make the select group. I was really hoping to be selected, and it fulfills one of my greatest dreams. I had a great time playing for the U.S. Team at the Los Angeles Games in 1984, and going back for a second shot is extra special."

The one-time St. John's University star, Mullin is something special himself. He works hard every minute of every night, but his work ethic wouldn't mean much if he weren't a sharpshooter from all angles of the court.

There's nothing flashy about Mullin's game. In fact, it's fairly predictable. You could almost draw up his moves and watch him execute them during every contest. Nevertheless, he remains one of the NBA's most effective players night in and night out. And for a shooter like Chris, the international three-point line—3 feet 3 inches closer to the basket than the NBA line—was sure to make him an even bigger threat.

Most important to the Olympic coaches, Mullin never gets out of shape. His conditioning is a key to his performance. But it wasn't always that easy.

Christopher Paul Mullin arrived at Golden State as the team's first-round choice—the seventh player selected—in the 1985 NBA draft. He came to California with a bushel of honors to his credit. Perhaps the greatest was the John Wooden Award, which goes to the nation's top college player. Mullin was also the co-Player of the Year in the Big East Conference, sharing the award with his Olympic (1984 and 1992) teammate Patrick Ewing. He was on top.

But not for long. Chris's first two pro years were just so-so. He missed 27 games in his rookie season and wound up averaging just 14 points per game. Although he played the full 82-game schedule in his second year, averaging 15.1 points per outing, he still wasn't playing like the Chris Mullin everyone remembered from St. John's. Something was wrong.

As it turned out, something was very wrong: Chris was an alcoholic. "I was lost," he says now. "I was confused. There were an awful lot of things I could have handled, but I didn't. I don't spend a lot of time looking back, but it's still fresh in my mind."

On December 12, 1987, Chris checked into an alcohol rehabilitation center in Inglewood, California. He spent almost a month there confronting his problem. "When I checked out of rehab," he recalls, "I was a new person. I had left my old self behind."

Mullin got right back to work, vowing to channel all of his energies into sculpting a new body, attitude, and life. The results were dramatic. He lost 30 pounds, gained a positive outlook, and finally started playing like a real first-round draft choice.

The record books should draw a line through Mullin's career stats. Below the line—after rehab—the numbers are amazing. From 1988-89 through 1991-92, Mullin averaged 25 points per game, played in four All-Star Games, averaged two steals a game—which puts him among the league leaders—and shot 54% from the field and 84% from the foul line. Early in his career, Mullin trade rumors floated by weekly. Now, he's as close to an untouchable as there is in the league.

Did anyone notice the change in Chris? Not anyone, everyone. Listen to Magic Johnson: "When God made basketball, He said to himself, 'I'm going to make a basketball player.' And the Lord went to work and carved out Chris Mullin. I have an incredible amount of respect for Chris. He has done so much with his life."

Mullin's game is deceptive. You can watch all night and barely notice him. You think he isn't doing much. Then you check the stat sheet and find he's got 30 points, a dozen assists, and three or four steals. It's amazing.

On the court, there's hardly a wasted motion from Chris. And he's smart, too. If the jumper isn't going, he concentrates on rebounding. If his team needs defense, he does a super job at that, poking the ball away from any opponent who doesn't pay 100 percent attention.

Why would a player who has so much going for him care about a second trip to the Olympics?

"It's just a matter of respect, I guess," says Chris. "Though I'm delighted to be in the select 10, I'd have been happy if they'd just mentioned me in the top 20. To me, the Olympic nomination means two things: a chance to represent my country and recognition that I'm near the top of my profession."

Slick from French Lick— LARRY BIRD

The 1992 Olympic Games may well be Larry Bird's last chance to fly. A serious back problem has kept the superstar out of the Boston Celtics' lineup frequently during recent seasons and his future seems uncertain. The way most folks see it, though, Bird would have been named to the U.S. Olympic team even if he'd have to have played in a wheelchair. The NBA owes him.

In the late 1970s, the National Basketball Association was in deep trouble. Many teams were losing money, and several were on the verge of going out of business. Enter Larry Joe Bird and Magic Johnson . . . and within years the NBA was the most successful league in all of professional sports.

Ever since he arrived in high school, Larry has been one rare Bird. A superstar at Springs Valley High School in his native Indiana, Bird was recruited by Indiana U. and its outspoken coach, Bob Knight. Larry had a hard time adjusting to college life—he was homesick and incompatible with Knight. He lasted only weeks at the university before returning home to French Lick in September 1974.

After checking his choices and waiting a year, Larry cast his lot with Indiana State in Terre Haute. ISU was a basketball unknown—until Bird came along and averaged 32.8 and 30.0 points per game in his first two seasons. Then, with a reasonable supporting cast, Bird led the Sycamores to an undefeated season and a miraculous berth in the Final Four. Only Magic and his Michigan State Spartans kept Bird's bunch from the national crown. The Bird-Johnson matchup drew a record TV crowd, setting the stage for an intense rivalry that would carry the NBA to its greatest heights.

Still, some pro scouts had doubts about Bird's pro potential. They felt that he was too slow. They also felt that he couldn't jump, and his shooting was marginal. But Boston boss Red Auerbach thought otherwise. Because Bird's original class at Indiana U. was graduating in 1978, Larry was eligible for the NBA draft that season, even though he'd already announced he was going back to his college, Indiana State, that year to finish his education. So Auerbach and the Celtics gambled that Bird was as good as they thought—and that they should sign before the 1979 NBA draft.

It was Red's best bet ever. Just before the 1979 selections, Larry signed a Celtic contract—and the rest, as they say, is history. Bird was an instant impact player, scoring 21.3 points and more than 10 rebounds per game. He proved to be one of the most imaginative passers the league had ever seen. At the end of his rookie season, Bird was Rookie of the Year. But for this superstar, it was just the start of things.

Bird might well have earned the nickname, "Mr. Triple Double." During the mid-1980s he regularly reached double figures (ten or more) in scoring, rebounds, and assists. Though foot injuries and back ailments frequently curtailed his playing time and output, Larry has remained a threat to lead his team in every category. On March 15, 1992, for example, playing only his eighth game after a long layoff, Bird beat the best of the West, the Portland Trail Blazers, 152-148, in double overtime. It was vintage Bird—a season-high 48 points along with 12 assists and 14 rebounds. At the end of regulation time, Larry sliced between two Blazer defenders and tossed in a big three-pointer at the buzzer to tie the score. At age 35, when he might have been playing out his time on a past dazzling record, Bird was still hustling like a kid.

With his career winding down, Larry has already passed the 21,000 career scoring mark with an average of more than 24 points per game. He's won virtually every honor the sport offers, including ten All-NBA selections, two playoff MVP awards (1984 and 1986), and another MVP award for the '82 All-Star Game.

Even playing at less than top level, Bird makes the Celtics go. Sure, he may lag behind on the fast break. Sure, he may not score inside like he once did. But his mere presence makes the team better. And he still has an uncanny knack for knocking down three-pointers, even with an opponent or two draped across his ailing back.

When Larry Bird finally decides to hang it up, they'll hoist jersey #33 to the top of Boston Garden. There it will join the rest of the green shirts whose owners made the Celtics the NBA's premier team for the last three decades. But there will always be something special about #33. If the next Larry Bird is out there waiting to strut his stuff, he hasn't shown up yet. The wait may be a long one.

The Admiral— DAVID ROBINSON

When young David Robinson arrived at the United States Naval Academy in Annapolis in 1983, he was 6 feet 7 inches tall, just one inch under the limit for entering plebes (freshmen). Any taller and a future naval officer would be too large to enter fighter planes and submarines. The height rule has always been a problem for Navy's basketball coaches, who quite naturally are inclined to think, "The bigger the better!" Imagine their reaction when David broke his hand while boxing that year and the Navy doctor who examined his X-rays announced, "This young man is going to grow some more." In fact, by the time David left the Academy in 1987, he was 7 feet 1 inch tall, and the greatest hoop star in Navy history. He then went on to become one of the most remarkable athletes in the NBA.

The son of a Navy man, David's early interests were mostly academic. They included science and electronics. Music was one of his hobbies—he did not study it, but he enjoyed playing it. Sports weren't high on his list. "When my dad was home [Mr. Robinson was frequently away for six months at a time on submarine duty], we did lots of family things," David recalls. "We'd go bowling or fishing together." But David's basketball was limited to neighborhood pick-up games. Organized leagues weren't his thing; in fact, he didn't play his first official game of basketball until he was a senior in high school.

David made his high-school team the first time he tried out but quit when he got tired of sitting on the bench. How could the coach know that this tiny 5-foot 5-inch 14-year-old kid would grow up to be a towering NBA center?

A combination of factors finally put Robinson on the basketball court. In 1982 his father retired from the Navy and moved the family to northern Virginia. By then, David had grown to 6 feet 6 inches, and was just the kind of young man that Art Payne, the coach at Osbourn Park High School, was looking for. "I only hoped he would like basketball," Payne remembers. Actually, David would have preferred gymnastics, but he decided to give basketball his best shot.

His great high school grades and excellent entrance exam scores earned David a Presidential appointment (there are only 100 per year) to the Naval Academy where there are about 4,100 students overall. The broken hand he'd gotten while boxing limited David's basketball production to only 7.6 points per game as a plebe. But that summer he played ball every day and lifted weights to put 20 pounds of muscle on his long, lean frame.

"If I'm going to play basketball," said David, "I'm going to be the best I can be." Like everything else he tried, Robinson worked to achieve his goal. Early in his sophomore year, he put together games of 31 and 37 points to help Navy win the Saluki Shootout tournament in Carbondale, Illinois. "I don't think anybody was as surprised as I was," David remembers. "I quickly realized what I might be able to do on a basketball court."

So did coach Paul Evans. "Not many guys his size had great hands, could shoot from outside, and run the floor," says Evans. And when Navy finished the '84 season with a super 26-6 record, all eyes were suddenly on this big fellow who had been playing the game for only three years.

Overnight, David had an important decision to make. If he stayed at Navy, he would owe his nation at least two years of military service after graduation. If he left at that point, he could turn pro right after college. David stayed. "My dad was a Navy man," he explains, "and I considered it a privilege to serve. Basically, I stayed at Navy to learn. No one can ever regret that."

David's basketball continued to improve—and so did Navy's. In his junior year, the Midshipmen went 30-5 as Robinson set a new NCAA record with 207 blocked shots. The team was 30-5 again in his senior year when David scored 50 points against Michigan and wound up with a Navy career high total of 2,669 points. That made him the only player in NCAA history to accumulate more than 2,500 points, 1,300 rebounds, and a 60% or higher shooting percentage.

When the 1987 NBA draft rolled around, there was no doubt that David Robinson was the prime pick. But would a team be willing to wait two years while he put in his Navy time? The San Antonio Spurs answered with a rousing "Yes!" They made David the top selection in the draft and held tight when he left for basic training in Georgia. While big men like Patrick Ewing were drawing $36,000 a game, David was pocketing his salary of $1,500 a month in the Navy!

David did interrupt his Navy career briefly when he was recruited for the 1988 Olympics, but when he failed to play like a superstar (12.8 points, 6.8 rebounds per game), some people in San Antonio began to wonder if he was really worth waiting for.

As it turned out, David quickly showed he was up to the high standards of the NBA when he entered the league in 1989. "Ever since I started playing serious basketball at the Academy," he said, "I've been highly motivated. I want to be considered with the best, and that takes hard work. That has never been a problem for me."

By the end of the 1989-90 season, David had proved his point. He turned the Spurs around completely: the team's 56-26 record was 35 games better than their previous season's 21-61, the biggest improvement in NBA history. It came as no surprise that Robinson was the unanimous choice for Rookie of the Year with his average of 24.3 points, 3.9 blocks, and 12 rebounds per game.

"If he's still learning how to play this game," said Mookie Blaylock of the Nets, "I'd hate to see him when he has it down cold." Coach Larry Brown agreed: "Rarely have I seen such speed, grace, and quickness in a 7 foot 1 inch player."

As Blaylock had feared, Robinson was just beginning. In his second season David averaged 25.6 points per outing and scored more than 40 points 3 times and more than 30 points 21 times. He also led the league in both rebounding and shot-blocking, an all-around effort that earned him first-team All-NBA honors and All-Defensive awards as well.

But even with all his athletic success, education has remained a major focus of David's life. He donates a great deal of time and money to various organizations that help young children. He also adopted one fifth-grade class at a San Antonio elementary school, establishing an endowment which will pay $2,300 per student when they graduate from high school.

On the court and off, David Robinson is a big man.

Out of the Shadows—SCOTTIE PIPPEN

Though pencil-thin Scottie Pippen doesn't cast a very large shadow of his own, he spent his first three years as a pro in the big shadow of one of basketball's greatest—his teammate Michael Jordan. Jordan was always the center of attention when the Chicago Bulls came to town, but increasingly it's been Pippen who's made the difference for one of the NBA's top teams.

"When we played Chicago," says Detroit Piston and Olympic coach Chuck Daly, "we used to double up on Michael and not worry about it. But now that Pippen has stepped forward and become a threat on his own, you just can't ignore him."

That's precisely what Bulls general manager Jerry Krause was counting on when he used a high first-round pick on the almost unknown Pippen in the 1987 NBA draft. Actually, Seattle chose Pippen with the fifth choice at the selection meeting, but a deal with Chicago had already been struck: the Bulls got the rights to Pippen in exchange for the rights to Olden Polynice, a second-round draft pick, plus a future first-round position swap. At the time that was a lot to give away, and NBA insiders wondered if Krause had taken leave of his senses.

"I guess you could call it a risk," says Krause. "If Scottie didn't turn out to be the player I thought he'd be, I'd have been criticized in every paper in the country." But there was method to Krause's madness. Game after game, he'd watched Chicago's rivals focus their defensive attention on Jordan. That should have left room for some of the other Bulls to score, but Jordan's teammates couldn't seem to take full advantage of the situation. Certainly Jordan had proved he could carry a team; but without help, the Bulls would never be champions. Enter Pippen, a young greyhound who could take the scoring pressure off Michael.

Unlike many superstars who earned national recognition as high-school players, Scottie was truly an unknown soldier. Though he played basketball at Hamburg High School in rural Hamburg, Arkansas, no one predicted a pro future for Pippen. At 6 feet 1 inch and only 145 pounds, he wasn't strong enough to do much on the court. When Scottie was only 15, his dad suffered a stroke and was confined to a wheelchair.

To help out, Scottie chose to stay close to home after his high-school days. He opted for the University of Central Arkansas in Conway, about 30 miles from Little Rock, where he was student-manager of the basketball team.

Then two things happened to change Scottie's life. First, a series of injuries depleted the Central Arkansas roster. The coach was forced to use Scottie as a player. In 20 games, the future NBA star averaged just 4.3 points per game. That's when the second thing happened. Scottie started growing . . . and growing . . . and growing. By the end of Scottie's freshman year in college, the 1983-84 season, he stood 6 feet 7 inches—and was on his way toward small-college stardom. Over his last three seasons he averaged more than 20 points per game, and finally attracted some attention from pro basketball's talent scouts.

But even though his value rose during the post-season all-star games that give small-college players a chance to strut their stuff against the big boys, Pippen was still considered a second-round pick by most experts. And then Jerry Krause stepped in.

After a so-so rookie year with the Bulls, Pippen blossomed during 1988-89. It was no accident that the Bulls did too. Although Jordan continued to light up the scoreboard and hit the key buckets, Pippen began functioning as a pressure valve, and the Bulls began looking like a championship-caliber team.

Scottie doesn't dominate the boards like Charles Barkley or Karl Malone. He doesn't score like Dominique Wilkins (when he's not suffering from physical problems). But in his own special way, Scottie does it all. One of the best defensive players in the game and a premier assist man on offense, Pippen is one of the few small forwards who gets the job done at both ends of the floor.

"I think I can do a lot of things," says Pippen. "I can handle the ball, rebound, defend, and score. I've got all of the tools."

Bulls coach Phil Jackson couldn't agree more. "Scottie must be an offensive force for us to win. He's a featured part of our offense. If the opponents don't concentrate on him, he's going to rip them apart." Jackson is also wise enough to assign Pippen to the other team's best offensive player. He usually leads the league's forwards in steals, and no other forward of his size blocks more shots than he does.

Playing with Michael Jordan could be a frustrating experience for anyone with ego problems, but fortunately for the Bulls, Pippen doesn't suffer from those. "You've got to take a lot of pride in what you do," he says. "You know you have to take a back seat to Michael, but you always want to stay competitive."

Playing with Jordan, however, has created one problem for Scottie. Like many other starters who play on teams with dominant superstars, Pippen was always snubbed when it came to the NBA All-Star Game. The experience left him somewhat bitter. "I did everything I could as a player," he says. "It obviously wasn't enough." The fans, however, finally came through and voted him to the East's starting lineup in 1992.

Coaches are always on the lookout for players who rise to the occasion. When the Bulls captured the 1991 Eastern Conference regular-season championship, Scottie averaged 17.8 points and 8 rebounds per game. In the post-season, as the Bulls stampeded to their first NBA title, he upped his scoring to 21.6 points per game. In the crucial fifth and final game against the Lakers, Scottie led all scorers with 32 points. That's coming up big in the clutch, which is exactly what the Olympic selection committee was hoping he would do when they tapped Scottie Pippen for the 1992 Games.

Mr. Point Guard—JOHN STOCKTON

Watching TV at Jack & Dan's Tavern in Spokane, Washington, can be a bit predictable. That's because, whenever possible, the set is tuned to basketball and, most of the time, it means that the Utah Jazz's John Stockton is playing somewhere. Oh, by the way, the owner of Jack & Dan's is Jack Stockton, John's dad.

When the Jazz selected John as the 16th pick of the first round in the 1984 NBA draft, most Utah fans had never heard of him. But John Stockton is the Babe Ruth of point guards. Before the 1988-89 NBA season, only two players—Kevin Porter and Isiah Thomas—had ever dished off more than 1,000 assists in a single season. And only Thomas had topped 1,100. But the old record was just the beginning for 6 foot 1 inch, 175-pound Stockton. Coming into the 1992 NBA campaign, John had put together four straight seasons with *at least* 1,128 assists and set a new record with 1,164. During the same four seasons, he had a hand—scoring or assisting—on 56.6% of all baskets scored by the Jazz.

The John Stockton story is something of a Cinderella tale. In Spokane, Washington, which is not exactly a hotbed of basketball activity, he was the smallest, skinniest kid in his neighborhood. Nevertheless, he was one of the best players in the Catholic Youth Organization program at St. Aloysius Elementary School, and his biggest dream was to make the varsity at nearby Gonzaga Prep. Watching him play on the ninth-grade team, Prep coach Terry Irwin figured that Stockton might be good enough to make the team by his senior year. He figured wrong. John worked hard and made it as a sophomore!

"John has a unique ability to forget a bad play or a good play right away," says Irwin, "and keep right on going." (He believes that what's done is done.) "When you add his incredible competitiveness and his work ethic, you know you've got a winner."

The nation's collegiate basketball powers somehow never discovered this little, 5-foot 4-inch kid in Spokane; so, with few other choices, John picked up his gear and moved across the street to Gonzaga University. No threat to make the NCAA Final Four, Gonzaga was best known as the alma mater of singer Bing Crosby.

Stockton's grandfather also happened to have qualified as a noteworthy alumnus: even though the school had dropped football years earlier, its best player back then had been Houston Stockton, John's grandfather, who went on to a short pro career.

How did John overcome his shortcomings? He simply outworked everyone. "He works hard at basketball," says Gonzaga coach Dan Fitzgerald. "Some guys don't do that. The one thing he really likes to do is play basketball."

John was good enough at Gonzaga to catch the attention of more than a few eyes. After being chosen for the coaches' All-Star Game in Seattle, he was invited by head coach Bob Knight to try out for the 1984 U.S. Olympic team. He just missed making it. Among the final cuts (the others included Charles Barkley and Terry Porter), Stockton remembers it as one of his biggest disappointments.

"I'm not sure I really expected to make the team," he says. "But when you get as close as I did, not making it was a pretty tough pill to swallow."

Stockton quickly put his disappointment behind him when he joined the Jazz that fall. During his first five pro seasons, he played in every game—82 per season. And gradually, his playing time increased.

Perhaps the best thing that ever happened

to Stockton was the arrival, in 1985, of Karl Malone. Another 1984 Olympic cut, Malone brought the inside game that so neatly complemented a ballhandler like Stockton. And Malone is quick to acknowledge that his standing among the NBA's top scorers owes much to the passing of John Stockton.

"He's like another coach out there," says longtime rival Fat Lever. "He simply doesn't make a lot of mistakes. He always controls the ball and, when it gets down to crunch time, he's always going to be out there."

Respect is the key to John's performance. "He demands discipline in running from the offensive sets," says Lever, "and he gets it. His teammates do what he tells them to do because they respect his knowledge and his ability."

Stockton's game has changed with time. When he got to the NBA, he was strictly a passer. Now, even though he's still a passer first, he also works to create—and take—his own shots. And Stockton is not a one-way player. He's equally effective on defense. Every year he's among the league leaders in steals, and he constantly bothers enemy ballhandlers. NBA opponents report that John has a trick of faking one way on defense, then coming back to strip the ball. He may not be fast, but he *is* quick to make the most of the talent available to him.

Even as an NBA All-Star, an Olympian, and a wealthy young man, Stockton never forgets what got him there. Hard work. "I may take a month or so off during the summer," he says, "but that's it. I can't sit back and then try to just turn it back on like some of the more talented guys. I've got to outwork them." John lives by a simple philosophy: "If you aren't practicing, someone else is."

In the Pressure Cooker—COACH CHUCK DALY

The good news for Chuck Daly was being named coach of the Olympic basketball team. After all, who wouldn't want to coach the best of the best? But the bad news for Chuck Daly was being named coach of the 1992 U.S. Olympic basketball team. No coach in the history of the sport ever had a tougher challenge. No coach had ever been expected to win a world championship so easily.

The man was tremendously well-prepared, of course. Everywhere he'd coached, Daly had succeeded. From high school through college and on to the pros, Chuck had won everywhere, often with less than the best talent. With the Olympic appointment, however, the dapper coach of the Detroit Pistons was presented with some of the greatest players ever to touch a basketball. The most critical eyes of the sports world would be clearly focused on his team.

It was a long road to the Olympics for Chuck Daly. A graduate of Bloomsburg University in Pennsylvania, he coached on the high-school level before making a name for himself as an assistant coach at Duke from 1963 to 1969. His performance there earned him his first college head coaching assignment, two seasons at Boston College (1969-1971). Then it was on to the University of Pennsylvania for six seasons, during which the Quakers went 125-38, a spectacular .767 winning percentage.

When Billy Cunningham was hired to coach the Philadelphia 76ers, he knew he needed help. Billy had never been a head coach before, so he looked across town and plucked his friend Daly off the Penn campus.

Chuck stayed in Philly for more than four years, but when the Cleveland Cavaliers called during the 1981-82 season, he thought he'd move on. Bad move. Even Chuck Daly couldn't help the hapless Cavaliers. They went 9-32 (a 22 percent victory pace) during Daly's brief half-season stay, and Chuck joined an ever-growing list of ex-Cav coaches. But Chuck wasn't finished yet. In fact, his best days were yet to come.

Daly had to wait out the next season, but in 1983-84 he took over the Detroit Pistons and began a nine-season string of incredible successes through 1991-92, never winning fewer than 46 games, never missing the NBA playoffs, and winning back-to-back NBA titles in 1989 and 1990. Only three coaches in league history had managed to do that.

Under Daly, defense became the Pistons' hallmark. Their half-court offense was workmanlike. Certainly they liked to run the ball when they could. But Detroit rose to the top of the NBA with an in-your-shirt defense, led by players like Isiah Thomas, Joe Dumars, and rebounding king Dennis Rodman. That's the style the Olympic leaders saw when they made Chuck their main man for 1992.

"Obviously I'm honored to have been selected as the head coach of the 1992 Olympic team," said Daly. "Frankly, the people at USA Basketball could have selected lots of people who were at least as qualified to do this job. But despite the obvious pressure, I'm delighted to take the challenge of bringing back the gold."

The Bonus Picks—CLYDE DREXLER and CHRISTIAN LAETTNER

When it comes to choosing up sides for a playground basketball game, you don't worry about who you pick for your eleventh and twelfth players. When it comes to selecting an Olympic team, however, numbers 11 and 12 can be mighty important.

So in early May 1992 when the U.S. Olympic basketball selection committee named Clyde Drexler of the Portland Trail Blazers and Christian Laettner of Duke University to the final two spots on the squad, basketball fans cheered. With the uncertainty produced by Magic Johnson's HIV-positive condition and Larry Bird's persistent back problems, these last two Olympic slots became even more important than they appeared to be when the original ten-man Dream Team was selected.

For Clyde Drexler, being chosen an Olympian was testimony that he had arrived at the top of his game. Throughout his career, Drexler's teams had earned shots at basketball's top prizes—but they kept coming up short. In college, his University of Houston Cougars were favored to win the 1983 NCAA title; then a last-second put-back by North Carolina State's Lorenzo Charles ended that dream. Later, when the Blazers seemed on the verge of winning NBA championships in 1990 and 1991, they came up a couple of games short.

Not that the shortfalls bother Drexler. He's one of the calmest players in the league. "We've had a shot at the championship rings," he says. "How many players ever come that close?"

What makes Drexler's attitude all the more remarkable is that he plays with more flair and style than anyone in the game—except maybe Michael Jordan. He floats, he flies, he scoops, and he dishes. During the 1991-92 season, he was the only player in the NBA to lead the loop in both scoring average and assists. He was also the Blazers' top man in steals, and he finished second in three-pointers and third in blocks and rebounds. That kind of performance figured to earn him his first—and long overdue—first-team All-NBA selection.

But Drexler didn't get to the top without a lot of hard work—including seven-day-a-week workouts. When he first arrived in the NBA, he brought along some pretty heavy baggage. He played out of control, according to some scouting reports, and his outside shooting was questionable. Add weak ballhandling to that, and decision-making skills that were, at best, unreliable.

But no more. Now Drexler hits the bull's-eye from the outside, dishes off with the best in the game, and takes sensible shots—most of the time.

Though he's very private about his personal life, Drexler's a leader off-court too. He chairs a Trail Blazer group called BASIC, which gives students incentives to improve on their academic skills.

Christian Laettner, unlike Drexler, grabbed the championship brass ring whenever the opportunity arose. Laettner led his Duke team to the NCAA's Final Four in each of his four seasons with the Blue Devils. At the 1992 championship tournament in Minnesota, he and his mates won their second straight title, thus becoming the first team since UCLA to win in consecutive seasons—1972 and 1973.

There's nothing flashy about Laettner's game, but the 6-foot 11-inch powerhouse from Buffalo, New York, was certainly the most versatile big man in college roundball. He was equally at home mixing it up under the boards or knocking down three-pointers from downtown. When things got tough for the Blue Devils, Laettner was the go-to guy. In the 1990 East regional finals against Connecticut, Christian's 15-footer at the final buzzer sent Duke to the Final Four. In March 1992, history repeated. With two seconds left in overtime in the regional final against Kentucky, Laettner put up a shot with exactly three-tenths of a second to go. He hit nothing but net, and again sent Duke to the finals—and its second title.

The success of that desperation shot surprised no one—except Kentucky fans. Laettner finished the game with ten baskets on ten shots (including a three-pointer) and ten free throws on ten attempts. It doesn't get much better than that.

By the time Duke sewed up the national championship with a 71-51 victory over Michigan, Laettner had carved his name into the annals of college sports history. The title test was his 23rd NCAA tournament game, an all-time record, and his 407 career points set another all-time mark.

Such talent and skill make Laettner a prize on any team. He was destined to be among the first players to be taken in the NBA draft. And between him and Clyde Drexler, the U.S. Olympic selection committee rounded out the basketball Dream Team with a major dose of style, power, and flexibility.

Staying Home

From 1936 through 1988, it was almost always college players who made up the U.S. Olympic Team. Some of the squads were legendary, like the 1960 unit that featured Oscar Robertson, Jerry West, Jerry Lucas, and Walt Bellamy. That team of future NBA All-Stars ripped through eight opponents by an *average margin* of 42 points!

As other countries adopted "America's Game," however, competition grew keener. Finally in 1992 professionals were allowed to play, and the U.S. basketball establishment couldn't have been happier.

According to the agreement between USA Basketball and the NBA, only one or possibly two spots on the 12-man U.S. roster would go to collegians. That meant 10 or 11 college players who might have expected to compete in Barcelona would watch the games at home. Here's a quick look at the 1992 U.S. team that might have been:

The Big Men

Shaquille O'Neal, LSU: The Human Eraser blocked a record 11 shots in the opening round of the 1992 NCAA Tournament. A 24-point scorer, he occupies a tremendous amount of space in the middle.

Alonzo Mourning, Georgetown: After a slow start at Georgetown, Mourning blossomed in his senior year to become the dominant collegiate big man in the East, if not the whole country. And though he scored more than 21 points per game, he was even better on defense.

The Forwards

Jim Jackson, Ohio State: The nation's premier college forward, Jackson averaged nearly 23 points for the Buckeyes. He runs the floor well and is unstoppable on the break.

Don MacLean, UCLA: When coach Jim Harrick arrived in Los Angeles to turn around the Bruins' program, MacLean was the guy who made it happen. He's a top-notch three-point shooter who isn't afraid to mix it up inside, either.

Byron Houston, Oklahoma State: In the talent-laden Big Eight conference, Houston took the Cowboys to the top early in the 1992 season. His leaping ability will test the limits of buildings with low ceilings.

The Guards

Walt Williams, Maryland: On a talent-poor Terrapin team, 6-foot 8-inch guard Williams took charge every night. With seven straight 30-point games, Walt became the Terps' single-season scoring champ. His loyalty—he stayed at Maryland even after the Terps were put on probation for violating NCAA rules after his sophomore year—is unquestioned.

Anthony Peeler, Missouri: This 6-foot 4-inch guard ran the show for Coach Norm Stewart. In the supertough Big Eight, he was the one who kept the Tigers in the hunt.

Harold Miner, Southern California: The Trojans were known as Harold and His Friends as they finished a surprising second in the Pac 10. With an unlimited shooting range, Miner does absolutely everything with the basketball.

These eight players might well have formed the nucleus of the 1992 Olympic Team—if the rules hadn't been changed. As it turned out, most of them will have to wait until at least 1996 before they get their shot at Olympic basketball.

What Next?

As you read this book, the league's All-Star team, also known as the 1992 U.S. Olympic Team, will have either shown its total domination of world basketball, or the NBA will have taken—and lost—one of the biggest gambles in sports history.

By furnishing the spectacular talent for the 1992 Olympics, the NBA risked its reputation as the world's biggest league. If its talent doesn't prove to be clearly superior, the world may cast a suspicious eye at America's pros. Not only would that damage the league's image, but it would hit the NBA where it really hurts: in the pocketbook. As worldwide interest in NBA televised games would be reduced, so would the money paid to sponsor those telecasts.

Chances are, however, that the NBA will have won this gamble and won it big. A quick study of the talent available elsewhere in the world clearly indicates a gap as big as the Grand Canyon. A U.S. loss would rank among the biggest sports upsets of all time. For that to happen, all 12 U.S. players would need to have their individual worst days, all on the same day.

Of course, the NBA Olympic Team could suffer the same problem that the old-fashioned college Olympic Teams suffered: lack of coordination. Unlike international teams who play together all year round, the U.S. teams generally have about a week to practice playing together before the qualifying tournament, and then a month or so to get ready for the Olympics themselves. Many fans fear that's just not enough time.

But Magic Johnson, for one, thinks it is. "The timetable isn't perfect," the former Lakers' star admitted when the Olympic roster was announced. But then he added, "A team like ours would only need a week to get started playing together. And we'll get better every time we step onto the court."

Since each of the U.S. players is a superstar in his own club, there was some question as to whether the players would be willing to make the individual sacrifices necessary to produce a victory. But few experts doubted it.

"Before I coached my first NBA All-Star Game, I wondered how much these great stars would sacrifice for the good of the team," said Olympic coach Chuck Daly. "The answer is, a lot.

They were totally focused on a team effort. An Olympic gold medal should give them even more focus."

Bottom line: the 1992 U.S. Olympic Team figured to be under greater pressure than any American team since the tournaments began in 1936. And even though these players are accustomed to high-pressure situations, this would be something special. As Larry Bird put it, "I know this. I wouldn't want to be on a team that loses in the Olympics. They probably wouldn't be allowed back in the country."

But even assuming that the United States blows away the rest of the world in Barcelona, that still doesn't address the questions basketball experts have been debating ever since FIBA announced that pros could play in 1992.

Will boring basketball be a turn-off for the fans? When NBC advertised its expensive cable triplecast of the 1992 Games, basketball people wondered how many fans would pay serious money to watch America beat a team like . . . Saudi Arabia.

Good question. Worldwide interest in basketball soared after the Soviet victory over the United States at the 1972 Olympics in Munich. The outcome may have been controversial, but it still proved a point: someone besides the United States had a chance to win an Olympic basketball tournament. The Yugoslavs, the Brazilians, the

Cubans, and the other world hoop powers took heart from the Soviet win. That, in some measure, increased the NBA's popularity around the globe. But if the rest of world basketball figures it will never have a chance to beat the United States, they may simply lose interest.

If victory comes too easily, will NBA stars still want to play? Though the NBA six-month regular season ends in late April, most of the league's superstars are involved with playoffs that don't end until June. It's a long year. To turn around then and spend another two months preparing for and playing in the Olympic tournament places an enormous demand on these players, each of whom can easily afford to take a long and well-deserved vacation.

And yet in 1992, the best players in the league willingly extended their season for a chance at Olympic glory. Some of them—Jordan, Ewing, Robinson, Mullin—looked forward to a second Olympic trip. Others—Stockton, Malone, Barkley—who had been late cuts in their post-college Olympic tryouts, were thrilled to get a second chance.

The 1992 Games were unique for the U.S. pros, but things may be very different by 1996. If the U.S. wins easily because there isn't any interesting competition, it might be harder to get the NBA's Top Ten to play in the 1996 Games in Atlanta.

What happens in the future when the Games go south? Geography students should pay attention here. In the northern hemisphere—those areas north of the equator—the summer runs from late June to late September. When the Games are held in Barcelona or in Atlanta, they're scheduled for a 2½-week period somewhere between late July and early September.

But if the Olympics are ever scheduled for a location in the southern hemisphere, the timetable flip-flops. When the 1956 Olympics were played in Australia, the Games lasted until December 8. If a future Summer Olympics were scheduled for Rio de Janeiro, Brazil; Buenos Aires, Argentina; or Auckland, New Zealand, the Games would actually come in the midst of winter sports activity in the northern half of the world.

Would the NBA be willing to delay its season to accommodate an Olympic team that had to be away during part of the regular basketball season? Or would the players agree to skip the first month of the season for a chance at a gold medal? It doesn't seem likely. But fortunately, as of now, no southern hemisphere Olympics are scheduled for the near future.

Will the best NBA players continue to participate in the Olympics if the current selection process continues? Unlike past Olympics, when extensive trials were conducted to select the U.S. basketball team, the 1992 American roster was chosen by a committee. As expected, the omission of some players from the squad sparked huge controversy. Detroit's Isiah Thomas, Joe Dumars, and Dennis Rodman were all likely Olympic candidates, as was L.A.'s James Worthy.

The omission of Thomas produced the most heated post-selection discussion. The rumor mill reported that Jordan refused to play if Isiah was picked. Michael denied it. And bad feelings between Thomas and coach Chuck Daly, Thomas and Larry Bird, and Thomas and NBA management in general were also blamed for his absence on the Olympic roster. But whatever the reason, Thomas's exclusion seemed so unfair that teammate Bill Laimbeer threatened legal action to force the Olympic Committee to hold tryouts for the squad. If the controversy continues into 1996 and beyond, there could be a problem signing the top pros for Olympic duty.

But with that—and all the other potential problems—one thing is clear: in the world of hoops, the most talented players play in the NBA. So long as these pros support the U.S. Olympic effort by competing in the Olympic Games, the Americans' future seems good as gold!

Player Stats

PATRICK ALOYSIUS EWING

Born August 5, 1962 at Kingston, Jamaica. Height 7'00" Weight 240.
High School: Cambridge, Mass., Rindge & Latin.
College: Georgetown University, Washington, D.C.

Sea.	Team	G	FGA	FGM	FG%	FTA	FTM	FT%
85–86	—New York	50	814	386	.474	306	226	.739
86–87	—New York	63	1053	530	.503	415	296	.713
87–88	—New York	82	1183	656	.555	476	341	.716
88–89	—New York	80	1282	727	.567	484	361	.746
89–90	—New York	82	1673	922	.551	648	502	.775
90–91	—New York	81	1645	845	.514	623	464	.745
91–92	—New York	82	1525	796	.522	511	377	.738
	Career	520	9175	4862	.530	3463	2567	.741

	Rebounds							
Sea.	Off.	Def.	Tot.	Assts.	Stls.	Blks.	Pts.	Avg.
85–86	124	327	451	102	54	103	998	20.0
86–87	157	398	555	104	89	147	1356	21.5
87–88	245	431	676	125	104	245	1653	20.2
88–89	213	527	740	188	117	281	1815	22.7
89–90	235	658	893	182	78	327	2347	28.6
90–91	194	711	905	244	80	258	2154	26.6
91–92	228	693	921	156	103	245	1970	24.0
Career	1396	3745	5141	1101	625	1606	12293	23.6

MICHAEL JEFFREY JORDAN

Born February 17, 1963 at Brooklyn, N.Y. Height 6'06" Weight 198.
High School: Wilmington, N.C., Laney.
College: University of North Carolina, Chapel Hill, N.C.

Sea. Team	G	FGA	FGM	FG%	FTA	FTM	FT%
84-85—Chicago	82	1625	837	.515	746	630	.845
85-86—Chicago	18	328	150	.457	125	105	.840
86-87—Chicago	82	2279	1098	.482	972	833	.857
87-88—Chicago	82	1998	1069	.535	860	723	.841
88-89—Chicago	81	1795	966	.538	793	674	.850
89-90—Chicago	82	1964	1034	.526	699	593	.848
90-91—Chicago	82	1837	990	.539	671	571	.851
91-92—Chicago	80	1818	943	.519	590	491	.832
Career	589	13644	7087	.519	5456	4620	.847

	Rebounds							
Sea.	Off.	Def.	Tot.	Assts.	Stls.	Blks.	Pts.	Avg.
84-85	167	367	534	481	196	69	2313	28.2
85-86	23	41	64	53	37	21	408	22.7
86-87	166	264	430	377	236	125	3041	37.1
87-88	139	310	449	485	259	131	2868	35.0
88-89	149	503	652	650	234	65	2633	32.5
89-90	143	422	565	519	227	54	2753	33.6
90-91	118	374	492	453	223	83	2580	31.5
91-92	91	420	511	489	182	75	2404	30.1
Career	996	2701	3697	2407	1594	623	19000	32.3

KARL MALONE

Born July 24, 1963 at Summerfield, La. Height 6'09" Weight 256.
High School: Summerfield, La.
College: Louisiana Tech University, Ruston, La.

Sea. Team	G	FGA	FGM	FG%	FTA	FTM	FT%
85-86—Utah	81	1016	504	.496	405	195	.481
86-87—Utah	82	1422	728	.512	540	323	.598
87-88—Utah	82	1650	858	.520	789	552	.700
88-89—Utah	80	1599	809	.519	918	703	.766
89-90—Utah	82	1627	914	.562	913	696	.762
90-91—Utah	82	1608	847	.527	888	684	.770
91-92—Utah	81	1516	798	.526	865	673	.778
Career	570	10398	5458	.525	5318	3826	.719

	Rebounds							
Sea.	Off.	Def.	Tot.	Assts.	Stls.	Blks.	Pts.	Avg.
85-86	174	544	718	236	105	44	1203	14.9
86-87	278	577	855	158	104	60	1779	21.7
87-88	277	709	986	199	117	50	2268	27.7
88-89	259	594	853	219	144	70	2326	29.1
89-90	232	679	911	226	121	50	2540	31.0
90-91	236	731	967	270	89	79	2382	29.0
91-92	225	684	909	241	108	51	2272	28.0
Career	1681	4518	6199	1549	788	404	14770	25.9

EARVIN JOHNSON, JR.

Born August 14, 1959 at Lansing, Mich. Height 6'09" Weight 220.
High School: Lansing, Mich., Everett.
College: Michigan State University, East Lansing, Mich.

Sea.	Team	G	FGA	FGM	FG%	FTA	FTM	FT%
79–80	—Los Angeles	77	949	503	.530	462	374	.810
80–81	—Los Angeles	37	587	312	.532	225	171	.760
81–82	—Los Angeles	78	1036	556	.537	433	329	.760
82–83	—Los Angeles	79	933	511	.548	380	304	.800
83–84	—Los Angeles	67	780	441	.565	358	290	.810
84–85	—Los Angeles	77	899	504	.561	464	391	.843
85–86	—Los Angeles	72	918	483	.526	434	378	.871
86–87	—Los Angeles	80	1308	683	.522	631	535	.848
87–88	—Los Angeles	72	996	490	.492	489	417	.853
88–89	—Los Angeles	77	1137	579	.509	563	513	.911
89–90	—Los Angeles	79	1138	546	.480	637	567	.890
90–91	—Los Angeles	79	976	466	.477	573	519	.906
	Career	874	11657	6074	.521	5649	4788	.848

	Rebounds							
Sea.	Off.	Def.	Tot.	Assts.	Stls.	Blks.	Pts.	Avg.
79–80	166	430	596	563	187	41	1387	18.0
80–81	101	219	320	317	127	27	798	21.6
81–82	252	499	751	743	208	34	1447	18.6
82–83	214	469	683	829	176	47	1326	16.8
83–84	99	392	491	875	150	49	1178	17.6
84–85	90	386	476	968	113	25	1406	18.3
85–86	85	341	426	907	113	16	1354	18.8
86–87	122	382	504	977	138	36	1909	23.9
87–88	88	361	449	858	114	13	1408	19.6
88–89	111	496	607	988	138	22	1730	22.5
89–90	128	394	522	907	132	34	1765	22.3
90–91	105	446	551	989	102	17	1531	19.4
Career	1561	4815	8376	9921	1698	361	17239	19.7

CHARLES WADE BARKLEY

Born February 20, 1963 at Leeds, Ala. Height 6'06" Weight 253.
High School: Leeds, Ala.
College: Auburn University, Auburn, Ala.

Sea.	Team	G	FGA	FGM	FG%	FTA	FTM	FT%
84–85	—Philadelphia	82	783	427	.545	400	293	.733
85–86	—Philadelphia	80	1041	595	.572	578	396	.685
86–87	—Philadelphia	68	937	557	.594	564	429	.761
87–88	—Philadelphia	80	1283	753	.587	951	714	.751
88–89	—Philadelphia	79	1208	700	.579	799	602	.753
89–90	—Philadelphia	79	1177	706	.600	744	557	.749
91–92	—Philadelphia	75	1126	622	.552	653	454	.695
	Career	610	8712	5025	.577	5347	3920	.733

	Rebounds							
Sea.	Off.	Def.	Tot.	Assts.	Stls.	Blks.	Pts.	Avg.
84–85	266	437	703	155	95	80	1148	14.0
85–86	354	672	1026	312	173	125	1603	20.0
86–87	390	604	994	331	119	104	1564	23.0
87–88	385	566	951	254	100	103	2264	28.3
88–89	403	583	986	325	126	67	2037	25.8
89–90	361	548	909	307	148	50	1989	25.2
91–92	271	559	830	308	136	44	1730	23.1
Career	2688	4391	7079	2276	1007	606	14184	23.3

LARRY JOE BIRD

Born December 7, 1956 at West Baden, Ind. Height 6'09" Weight 220.
High School: French Lick, Ind., Springs Valley.
Colleges: Indiana University, Bloomington, Ind., Northwood Institute, West Baden, Ind., and Indiana State University, Terre Haute, Ind.

Sea.	Team	G	FGA	FGM	FG%	FTA	FTM	FT%
79–80—	Boston	82	1463	693	.474	360	301	.836
80–81—	Boston	82	1503	719	.478	328	283	.863
81–82—	Boston	77	1414	711	.503	380	328	.863
82–83—	Boston	79	1481	747	.504	418	351	.840
83–84—	Boston	79	1542	758	.492	421	374	.888
84–85—	Boston	80	1760	918	.522	457	403	.882
85–86—	Boston	82	1606	796	.496	492	441	.896
86–87—	Boston	74	1497	786	.525	455	414	.910
87–88—	Boston	76	1672	881	.527	453	415	.916
88–89—	Boston	6	104	49	.471	19	18	.947
89–90—	Boston	75	1517	718	.473	343	319	.930
90–91—	Boston	60	1017	462	.454	183	163	.891
91–92—	Boston	45	758	353	.466	162	150	.926
	Career	897	17334	8591	.496	4471	3960	.886

	Rebounds							
Sea.	Off.	Def.	Tot.	Assts.	Stls.	Blks.	Pts.	Avg.
79–80	216	636	852	370	143	53	1745	21.3
80–81	191	704	895	451	161	63	1741	21.2
81–82	200	637	837	447	143	66	1761	22.9
82–83	193	677	870	458	148	71	1867	23.6
83–84	181	615	796	520	144	69	1908	24.2
84–85	164	678	842	531	129	98	2295	28.7
85–86	190	615	805	557	166	51	2115	25.8
86–87	124	558	682	566	135	70	2076	28.1
87–88	108	595	703	467	125	57	2275	29.9
88–89	1	36	37	29	6	5	116	19.3
89–90	90	622	712	562	106	61	1820	24.3
90–91	53	456	509	431	108	58	1164	19.4
91–92	46	388	434	306	42	33	908	20.2
Career	1757	7217	8974	5695	1556	755	21791	24.3

DAVID MAURICE ROBINSON

Born August 6, 1965 at Key West, Fla. Height 7'01" Weight 235.
High School: Manassas, Va., Osbourn Park.
College: United States Naval Academy, Annapolis, Md.

Sea.	Team	G	FGA	FGM	FG%	FTA	FTM	FT%
89–90—	San Antonio	82	1300	690	.531	837	613	.732
90–91—	San Antonio	82	1366	754	.552	777	592	.762
91–92—	San Antonio	68	1074	592	.551	561	393	.701
	Career	232	3740	2036	.544	2175	1598	.735

	Rebounds							
Sea.	Off.	Def.	Tot.	Assts.	Stls.	Blks.	Pts.	Avg.
89–90	303	680	983	164	138	319	1993	24.3
90–91	335	728	1063	208	127	320	2101	25.6
91–92	261	568	829	181	158	305	1578	23.2
Career	899	1976	2975	553	423	944	5672	24.4

CHRISTOPHER PAUL MULLIN

Born July 30, 1963 at New York, N.Y. Height 6'07" Weight 215.
High School: Brooklyn, N.Y., Xaverian
College: St. John's University, Jamaica, N.Y.

Sea.	Team	G	FGA	FGM	FG%	FTA	FTM	FT%
85–86	Golden State	55	620	287	.463	211	189	.896
86–87	Golden State	82	928	477	.514	326	269	.825
87–88	Golden State	60	926	470	.508	270	239	.885
88–89	Golden State	82	1630	830	.509	553	493	.892
89–90	Golden State	78	1272	682	.536	568	505	.889
90–91	Golden State	82	1449	777	.536	580	513	.884
91–92	Golden State	81	1584	830	.524	420	350	.833
	Career	520	8409	4353	.518	2928	2558	.873

	Rebounds							
Sea.	Off.	Def.	Tot.	Assts.	Stls.	Blks.	Pts.	Avg.
85–86	42	73	115	105	70	23	768	14.0
86–87	39	142	181	261	98	36	1242	15.1
87–88	58	147	205	290	113	32	1213	20.2
88–89	152	331	483	415	176	39	2176	26.5
89–90	130	333	463	319	123	45	1956	25.1
90–91	141	302	443	329	173	63	2107	25.7
91–92	127	323	450	286	173	62	2074	25.6
Career	689	1651	2340	2005	926	300	11536	22.2

SCOTTIE PIPPEN

Born September 25, 1965 at Hamburg, Ark. Height 6'07" Weight 210.
High School: Hamburg, Ark.
College: University of Central Arkansas, Conway, Ark.

Sea.	Team	G	FGA	FGM	FG%	FTA	FTM	FT%
87–88	Chicago	79	564	261	.463	172	99	.576
88–89	Chicago	73	867	413	.476	301	201	.668
89–90	Chicago	82	1150	562	.489	295	199	.675
90–91	Chicago	82	1153	600	.520	340	240	.706
91–92	Chicago	82	1359	687	.506	434	330	.760
	Career	398	5093	2523	.495	1542	1069	.693

	Rebounds							
Sea.	Off.	Def.	Tot.	Assts.	Stls.	Blks.	Pts.	Avg.
87–88	115	183	298	169	91	52	625	7.9
88–89	138	307	445	256	139	61	1048	14.4
89–90	150	397	547	444	211	101	1351	16.5
90–91	163	432	595	511	193	93	1461	17.8
91–92	185	445	630	572	155	93	1720	21.0
Career	751	1764	2515	1952	789	400	6205	15.6

JOHN HOUSTON STOCKTON

Born March 26, 1962 at Spokane, Wash. Height 6'01" Weight 175.
High School: Spokane, Wash., Gonzaga Prep.
College: Gonzaga University, Spokane, Wash.

Sea.	Team	G	FGA	FGM	FG%	FTA	FTM	FT%
84–85	—Utah	82	333	157	.471	193	142	.736
85–86	—Utah	82	466	228	.489	205	172	.839
86–87	—Utah	82	463	231	.499	229	179	.782
87–88	—Utah	82	791	454	.574	324	272	.840
88–89	—Utah	82	923	497	.538	452	390	.863
89–90	—Utah	78	918	472	.514	432	354	.819
90–91	—Utah	82	978	496	.507	434	363	.836
91–92	—Utah	82	939	453	.482	366	308	.842
	Career	652	5811	2988	.514	2635	2180	.827

	Rebounds							
Sea.	Off.	Def.	Tot.	Assts.	Stls.	Blks.	Pts.	Avg.
84–85	26	79	105	415	109	11	458	5.6
85–86	33	146	179	610	157	10	630	7.7
86–87	32	119	151	670	177	14	648	7.9
87–88	54	183	237	1128	242	16	1204	14.7
88–89	83	165	248	1118	263	14	1400	17.1
89–90	57	149	206	1134	207	18	1345	17.2
90–91	46	191	237	1164	234	16	1413	17.2
91–92	68	202	270	1126	244	22	1297	15.8
Career	399	1234	1633	7365	1633	121	8395	12.8

CLYDE DREXLER

Born June 22, 1962 at New Orleans, La. Height 6'07" Weight 215.
High School: Houston, Tex., Sterling
College: University of Houston, Houston, Tex.

Sea.	Team	G	FGA	FGM	FG%	FTA	FTM	FT%
83–84	—Portland	82	559	252	.451	169	123	.728
84–85	—Portland	80	1161	573	.494	294	223	.759
85–86	—Portland	75	1142	542	.475	381	293	.769
86–87	—Portland	82	1408	707	.502	470	357	.760
87–88	—Portland	81	1679	849	.506	587	476	.811
88–89	—Portland	78	1672	829	.496	548	439	.799
89–90	—Portland	73	1357	670	.494	430	333	.774
90–91	—Portland	82	1338	645	.482	524	416	.794
91–92	—Portland	76	1476	694	.470	505	401	.794
Career		713	11792	5761	.489	3908	3060	.783

	Rebounds							
Sea.	Off.	Def.	Tot.	Assts.	Stls.	Blks.	Pts.	Avg.
83–84	112	123	235	153	107	29	628	7.7
84–85	217	259	476	441	177	68	1377	17.2
85–86	171	250	421	600	197	46	1389	18.5
86–87	227	291	518	566	204	71	1782	21.7
87–88	261	272	533	467	203	52	2185	27.0
88–89	289	326	615	450	213	54	2123	27.2
89–90	208	299	507	432	145	51	1703	23.3
90–91	212	334	546	493	144	60	1767	21.5
91–92	166	334	500	512	138	70	1903	25.0
Career	1863	2488	4351	4114	1528	501	14857	20.8

CHRISTIAN LAETTNER

Born: August 17, 1969 at Buffalo, N.Y. Height: 6'11" Weight: 235.
High School: The Nichols School, Buffalo, NY
College: Duke University, Durham, N.C.
First Round Selection June 1992 Draft

Sea. Team	G	FGA	FGM	FG%	FTA	FTM	FT%
88-89—Duke	36	159	115	.723	121	88	.727
89-90—Duke	38	380	194	.511	269	225	.836
90-91—Duke	39	471	271	.575	263	211	.802
91-92—Duke	35	442	254	.575	232	189	.815
Career		1452	834	.574	885	713	.806

	Rebounds							
Sea.	Off.	Def.	Tot.	Assts.	Stls.	Blks.	Pts.	Avg.
88-89	—	—	170	44	35	28	319	8.9
89-90	—	—	364	84	59	41	619	16.3
90-91	—	—	340	76	75	44	771	19.8
91-92	—	—	275	69	74	32	751	21.5
Career	—	—	1149	273	243	145	2460	16.6